WHOLE WIDE WORLD
CHICHÉN I

by Kristine

Ideas for Parents and Teachers

Pogo Books let children practice reading informational text while introducing them to nonfiction features such as headings, labels, sidebars, maps, and diagrams, as well as a table of contents, glossary, and index.

Carefully leveled text with a strong photo match offers early fluent readers the support they need to succeed.

Before Reading

- "Walk" through the book and point out the various nonfiction features. Ask the student what purpose each feature serves.
- Look at the glossary together. Read and discuss the words.

Read the Book

- Have the child read the book independently.
- Invite him or her to list questions that arise from reading.

After Reading

- Discuss the child's questions. Talk about how he or she might find answers to those questions.
- Prompt the child to think more. Ask: A pyramid is at the center of Chichén Itzá. Where else in the world can you find pyramids?

Pogo Books are published by Jump!
5357 Penn Avenue South
Minneapolis, MN 55419
www.jumplibrary.com

Library of Congress Cataloging-in-Publication Data

Names: Spanier, Kristine, author.
Title: Chichén Itzá / by Kristine Spanier, MLIS.
Description: Minneapolis, MN: Jump!, Inc., [2022]
Series: Whole wide world
Includes index. | Audience: Ages 7-10
Identifiers: LCCN 2021025151 (print)
LCCN 2021025152 (ebook)
ISBN 9781636903040 (hardcover)
ISBN 9781636903057 (paperback)
ISBN 9781636903064 (ebook)
Subjects: LCSH: Chichén Itzá Site (Mexico)–
Juvenile literature. | Mayas–Mexico–Yucatán (State)–
Rites and ceremonies–Juvenile literature.
Yucatán (Mexico: State)–Antiquities–Juvenile literature.
Classification: LCC F1435.1.C5 S65 2022 (print)
LCC F1435.1.C5 (ebook) | DDC 972/.65–dc23
LC record available at https://lccn.loc.gov/2021025151
LC ebook record available at https://lccn.loc.gov/2021025152

Editor: Jenna Gleisner
Designer: Molly Ballanger

Photo Credits: snem/iStock, cover; Liya_Blumesser/
Shutterstock, 1; lunamarina/Shutterstock, 3; CostinT/
iStock, 4; Pauws99/iStock, 5; Sergi Reboredo/Alamy, 6-7;
Iren Key/Shutterstock, 8; Jon G. Fuller/VWPics/Alamy, 9;
Jui-Chi Chan/iStock, 10-11; Stefano Ember/Shutterstock,
12-13; Heliopixel/Shutterstock, 14; Joseph Sohm/
Shutterstock, 14-15; Myroslava Bozhko/Shutterstock,
16-17; gallimaufry/Shutterstock, 18; Olga Gabay/
Shutterstock, 19; Matyas Rehak/Shutterstock, 20-21;
Lukiyanova Natalia frenta/Shutterstock, 23.

Printed in the United States of America at
Corporate Graphics in North Mankato, Minnesota.

TABLE OF CONTENTS

CHAPTER 1

· ·

ANCIENT CIVILIZATION

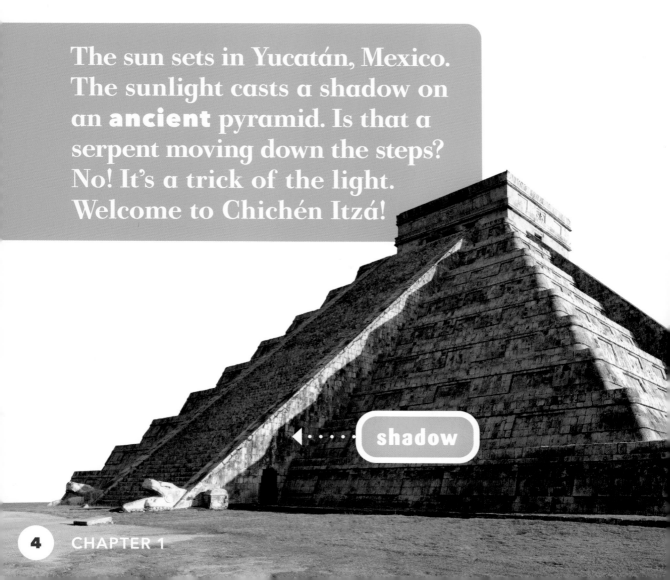

The sun sets in Yucatán, Mexico. The sunlight casts a shadow on an **ancient** pyramid. Is that a serpent moving down the steps? No! It's a trick of the light. Welcome to Chichén Itzá!

shadow

Chichén Itzá was once a **civilization**. Maya people settled here more than 1,500 years ago. Toltec people moved here about 500 years later. Pictures of them are carved in stone.

Chichén Itzá covers four square miles (10 square kilometers). At one point, about 50,000 people lived here. There are more than 20 buildings. They are all made of stone.

CHAPTER 2

· ·

STONE BUILDINGS

One of the buildings is an **observatory**. From it, the Maya people studied the stars. They used this knowledge to create calendars. This helped them track the passing of time.

◄ · · · · · **observatory**

Ceremonies took place at the Platform of the Skulls. Look closely. Carvings of skulls cover the sides.

Platform of the Skulls

The pyramid at the center of the site is the **Temple** of Kukulcan. It is 79 feet (24 meters) tall. Each side has 91 steps. The top platform adds another step. This totals 365 steps. That is the number of days in a year.

WHAT DO YOU THINK?

Kukulcan is a god from **myths**. The Maya and Toltec people **worshipped** him. Why do you think his pyramid is in the center of the site?

steps

Las Monjas

Chac carving

Las Monjas is one of the oldest buildings here. It may have been a government building. It is covered in carvings. Above the entrance is a carving of Chac. Chac was the god of rain.

DID YOU KNOW?

This area is hot and dry. Water is hard to come by. The Maya people put gifts in cenotes for Chac. Cenotes are **sinkholes**. They fill with water when it rains.

Statues of Chac are called Chac Mools. One is at the top of the Temple of the **Warriors**.

About 200 columns stand around the temple. Images of warriors are carved on them.

Chac Mool

Temple of
the Warriors

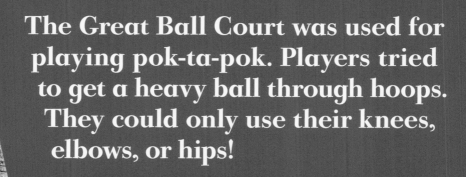

The Great Ball Court was used for playing pok-ta-pok. Players tried to get a heavy ball through hoops. They could only use their knees, elbows, or hips!

WHAT DO YOU THINK?

Pok-ta-pok was played with a ball. What other sports use a ball for scoring? Do you think pok-ta-pok would be hard to play? Why or why not?

CHAPTER 3
CHICHÉN ITZÁ TODAY

Chichén Itzá was **abandoned** around 1250. No one knows why. People from Spain arrived here in 1526. All that is left is **ruins**.

Visitors were once able to climb the pyramid steps.

TAKE A LOOK!

People have been visiting this area for more than 1,500 years. Take a look at some of the site's important dates.

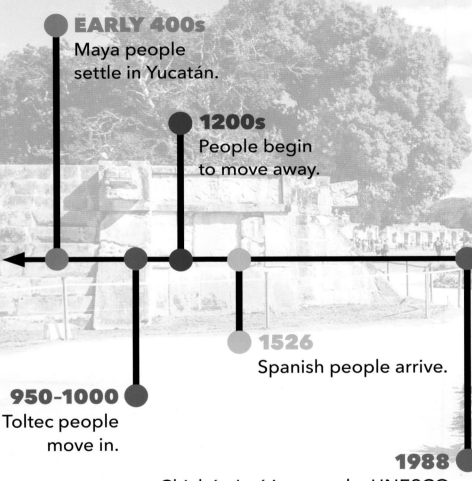

EARLY 400s
Maya people settle in Yucatán.

1200s
People begin to move away.

1526
Spanish people arrive.

950–1000
Toltec people move in.

1988
Chichén Itzá is named a UNESCO World Heritage site. People recognize its importance. They work to protect it.

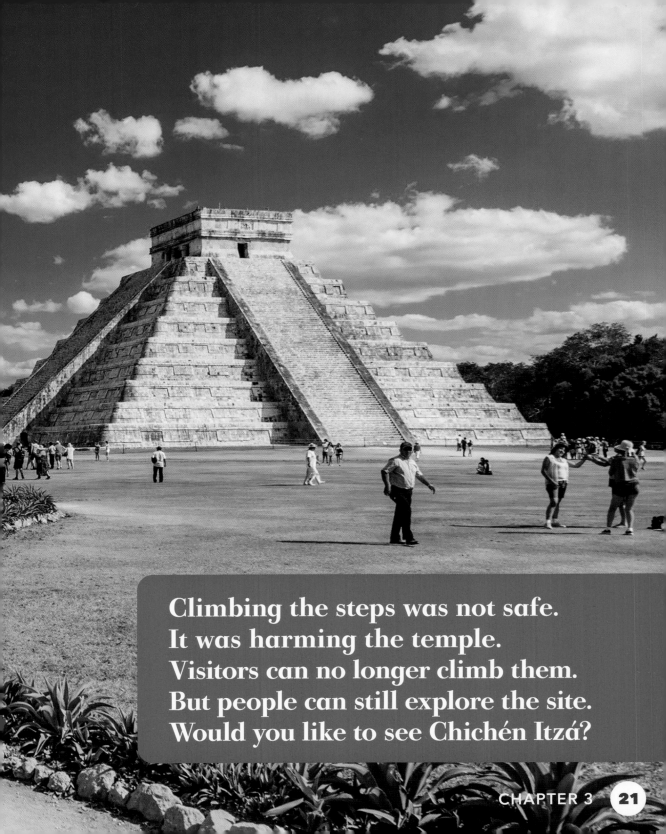

Climbing the steps was not safe.
It was harming the temple.
Visitors can no longer climb them.
But people can still explore the site.
Would you like to see Chichén Itzá?

QUICK FACTS & TOOLS

CHICHÉN ITZÁ

Location: Yucatán, Mexico

Size: four square miles
(10 square kilometers)

Years Built (estimate):
600 to 1000

Primary Builders:
Maya and Toltec people

Past Use: ceremonial site
and city

Current Use: cultural site
and visitor attraction

Number of Visitors Each Year:
around 2 million

GLOSSARY

abandoned: Left, never to be returned to.

ancient: Belonging to a period long ago.

ceremonies: Formal events that mark important occasions.

civilization: A developed and organized society.

myths: Old stories that express the beliefs or history of a group of people or explain natural events.

observatory: A building for studying the stars and weather.

ruins: The remains of something that has collapsed or been destroyed.

sinkholes: Natural holes in the ground in which water collects.

temple: A building used for worship.

warriors: Brave and experienced soldiers.

worshipped: Showed love and devotion to a god or gods, especially by praying or singing in a religious building with others.

INDEX

TO LEARN MORE

Finding more information is as easy as 1, 2, 3.

1 Go to www.factsurfer.com

2 Enter "ChichénItzá" into the search box.

3 Choose your book to see a list of websites.

FACT SURFER